Unity
in the
DIVERSITY
of
DIFFERENT
RELIGIONS

Fourth Edition

Unity in the DIVERSITY of DIFFERENT RELIGIONS

Fourth Edition

DALJIT SINGH JAWA

Unity in the Diversity of Different Religions by Daljit Singh Jawa
Fourth Edition

This book is written to provide information and motivation to
readers. Its purpose is not to render any type of psychological, legal,
or professional advice of any kind. The content is the sole opinion and
expression of the author, and not necessarily that of the publisher.

Printed in the United States of America.

ISBN 978-1-955363-42-6 (Paperback)
ISBN 978-1-955363-43-3 (Digital)

Lettra Press books may be ordered through booksellers or by contacting:

Lettra Press LLC
30 N Gould St. Suite 4753
Sheridan, WY 828011
1 307-200-3414 | info@lettrapress.com
www.lettrapress.com

CONTENTS

PREFACE

It is a common belief, that since very early times, man has been trying to struggle for his survival and sustenance. In this struggle, he had to deal with not only other living beings, but also the natural phenomena, such as rains, floods, and draughts.

For dealing with other animals and insects, and living in security, he developed various hand tools and weapons, and formed groups or tribes with his fellow human beings. But he could not do anything to save himself from the dangers and devastating effects of such natural calamities as torrential rains, high floods, and earthquakes.

Depending on the geographical area, and other historical and cultural factors, different people developed different theories and beliefs about these natural phenomena and started believing in different supernatural powers or gods, and then one ultimate or supreme power, who controlled even these lesser gods, and destinies of human beings. This gave birth to different systems of beliefs or religions in different parts of the world.

As is readily discernable from the recorded history, it is believed that in the east side of the globe, first developed the *Sanatan*, or *Hindu* faith. The Hindu faith gave birth to Jainism, Buddhism, and Sikhism. Similarly in the west, first developed Zorastarism, then Judaism, Christianity, and Islam. Then there are unaccountable branches and offshoots of these faiths.

During his lifetime, the author (a Sikh himself) had the opportunity of dealing with and interacting with members of many faiths, and at least briefly study their scriptures. Contrary to many misconceptions, propagated by the fanatics or the misinformed, he has found that even though people of different faiths, may dress differently, eat differently, or worship differently, yet at their core, they are generally good people, who want to love, and be loved, and that is what their holy scriptures and their prophets, messengers, and Gurus really teach. In other words, there is Unity in The Diversity of Different Religions.

This book is a humble attempt of the author to prove his above hypothesis, by taking appropriate quotes from the holy scriptures, and true or mythological stories from different faiths, and show the readers, how at their core, all religions, and traditions try to teach us virtues, such as love, compassion, and forgiveness, and remain away from vices, such as lust, greed, anger, and ego.

I hope the readers would find these quotes and stories worth sharing with others, particularly their children, so that they all grow to become good human beings themselves, and love and respect all their fellow humans, irrespective of their faiths, cultures, or traditions.

Daljit Singh Jawa
Jawa222@gmail.com.
June 2023

UNITY IN DIVERSITY OF DIFFERENT WORLD RELIGIONS

Paragraph 2 of the US declaration of Independence begins with the statement:

"We hold these truths to be self-evident, that all men are created equal, that they are endowed by their Creator with certain unalienable Rights, that among these are Life, Liberty and the pursuit of Happiness."

Probably, it was this pursuit of happiness, which motivated some chosen divinely wise men (prophets), born at different times, and different places to ponder and devise the best ways to achieve this goal. The sum total of these conclusions was later given a name and called a religion.

These divinely wise men (prophets), were born at different times in history, and in different parts of the world, so they had to state their philosophies or advice, keeping in mind the different circumstances, cultural habits, and ways of life of people in that particular time and context. Therefore, it is but natural, that on the surface, these world religions appear so very different, and have often been blamed for so much tension, discord, and even terrible wars, among countries and nations of the world.

But if we study different religions objectively, we would find that basically all major religions try to teach their followers, common basic values, such as honesty, truthful living, love, kindness, forgiveness, and compassion not only for their own families and friends, but also for their neighbors, and even their enemies. In fact, there is so much commonality, that we won't be too much amiss in saying that there is Unity in the Diversity of Different World Religions.

Following are some quotes, which show, how different religions emphasize the same core values. These quotes are copied from "World Scripture: A comparative Anthology of Sacred Texts," a project of the international Religious Foundation, (St. Paul, MN: Paragon House, USA, 1995).

Further, unless stated otherwise, the quotes regarding Sikhism, have been copied from the English translation of Sri Guru Granth Sahib (SGGS) by Sant Singh Khalsa.

As for the stories included in this book, these have been adapted from various Internet sites, sacred books, or what the author could recollect from the stories he read or heard during his teenager days. The author thanks all these sources, and has tried to mention these specifically, wherever he could.

LOVING-KINDNESS:

ALTHOUGH STATED IN DIFFERENT words, all major religions of the world, stress upon the quality of loving not just our own family and friends, but also our neighbors, irrespective of their faith, race, color, caste, or ethnicity. Some faiths even teach us, how not only to forgive our enemies, but also treat them with utmost kindness and compassion. This is evident from the following quotes from the scriptures, historical episodes, or legends from different faith traditions.

1. "Those who act kindly in this world will have kindness." (*Islam*, Qur'an 39.10).

2. What sort of religion can it be without compassion? You need to show compassion to all living beings, Compassion is the root of all religious faiths." (*Hinduism*, Basvani, Vacaana 247).

3. "Do not rebuke an older man, but exhort him as you would a father; treat younger men like brothers, older women like mothers, younger women like sisters, in all purity." (*Christianity*. 1. Timothy 5.1-2)
4. "Be kind to all beings, this is more meritorious than bathing at sixty-eight sacred shrines of pilgrimage and the giving of charity." (*Sikhism*, SGGS P. 136)
5. "The world stands upon three things: upon the Law, upon Worship, and upon showing Kindness." (Judaism, Mishnah, Abot 1.2)

1. Story Of Brother Ghannaeea

It was more than 300 years ago, when there was no Red Cross, or any other charitable organizations, which would take care of or provide any kind of relief to the soldiers wounded or severely incapacitated in a war. It was the time, when the most cruel and fanatic emperor, who had ascended to the throne after mercilessly killing his real brothers, and imprisoning his own father, was ruling India. The people of India were so terrorized, that no body dared to raise his or her voice against any of the cruel or unjust orders of this king, whether it related to the demolition of their places of worship, assaulting their women, or forcibly asking them to change their faiths.

Guru Gobind Singh, the tenth Guru (prophet) of the Sikhs, took the courage to stand against this despotic king, by organizing his followers into an army of saint soldiers. He advised them that in ordinary circumstances, they were to live like saints, always worshipping God, and living a life of love and compassion for all, but if some one unjustly attacked them, or tried to terrorize any innocent human being, then they should be prepared to defend themselves, and other innocent victims.

Once, it so happened that Guru Gobind Singh Ji was resting in his chambers, and a few sikhs (followers) were carrying on some casual conversation outside Guru Ji's chamber. But suddenly, they heard the noise of trotting of many horses, rising of dust, and the war cries of the king's soldiers quickly marching towards them.

The sikhs immediately realized, that some how the emperor's forces had found out that at this time Guru Gobind Singh is in a very vulnerable situation, and it will not be very difficult for them to kill a small number of his sikhs (followers), and capture the Guru alive, and then receive a handsome prize from the king.

But the devoted sikhs did not want to disturb their Guru with the news of this danger. So before the enemy soldiers could come nearer, all the Sikh men and women got hold of their arms, and went out to engage the enemy at a distance, and prevent them from reaching the Guru's chamber.

As expected a furious desperate battle ensued and the soldiers of both sides started being seriously wounded, or killed. While this carnage was going on an old Sikh named Ghannaeea, who had been assigned the duty to give water to the wounded Sikh soldiers, was running around and providing water not only to the Sikhs, but also to the enemy soldiers.

Although greatly outnumbered, the Sikh soldiers fought so fiercely and valiantly that the enemy soldiers soon started abandoning the battlefield, and finally ran away deserting even their dead and injured fellow soldiers to their own fate.

After making sure that there was no more danger to their Guru, the Sikhs happily started proceeding towards their Guru, eager to relate this happy news to him. But at the same time some of the Sikhs, who had noticed brother Ghannaeea giving water to the enemy soldiers, caught hold of him, and proceeded to report this seemingly "traitorous" act of his to the Guru.

After duly praising and blessing the Sikhs for their alertness in sensing the danger, commitment to their Guru, and bravery, Guru Ji took the case of brother Ghannaeea, and asked him, why he was giving water to the enemy soldiers, and thus helping them to rise again, and fight against the Sikhs.

Brother Ghannaeea calmly replied: "Guru Ji, I did not give any water to any Sikh or enemy soldier. I was giving water only to God."

When asked to explain, he said: "Guru Ji, you yourself have taught me, that we are all children of the same one God, and it is the same one God, who abides in all beings. Therefore, we should see God in each and every human being. So I was in effect giving water only to God, and I don't think, it is a crime to give a few drops of water to Him."

Hearing this reply, Guru Ji was so pleased, that taking out an ointment tube, he gave it to Ghannaeea, and said: " Dear brother Ghannaeea, you have truly enshrined my message of universal love in your heart. So from now on when you go to any battlefield, not only give water to all fallen and injured soldiers, but also apply ointment on their wounds, and provide other necessary first aid.

(Adapted from a true story in Sikh history)

2. Prophet Ali And His Mortal Enemy

Ali was the son –in –law of Muhammad, the first and the last prophet of Islam. Upon the death of prophet Muhammad, ignoring Ali, his followers first chose Abu Bakar, then Umar, and then Uthmaan as the next three Khalifas or heads of Islam. It was only in the fourth place that Ali was chosen as the new Khalifa.

Ali was a very noble, wise, and brave man. But there were many people who did not care about his qualities or his right to become Khalifa, and were always scheming to kill him, and have their own favored person chosen as the Khalifa.

However, unmindful of the danger from his enemies, Ali kept ruling his kingdom with justice, mercy, and compassion, and kept regularly going to the mosque in Kufa (Iraq) for his daily prayers. One day, when with bowed head, Ali was saying his *Namaz* (prayer), a man suddenly came from behind, and attacked him with a long poisoned knife, and then started running outside the mosque with a blood soaked knife in his hand.

Seeing this tragedy in front of them, some people immediately rushed to the aid of Ali, gave him first aid, and took him to his home for further treatment and comfort. In the mean time those who were outside the mosque, saw the assailant running with a blood soaked knife. They caught hold of him, and brought him also to Ali's house for severe punishment.

At that time Ali was resting on his bed, and was about to drink some milk to quench his thirst. Upon seeing his assailant, who naturally appeared very much afraid, terrified, and thirsty, Ali put down his glass. Then he asked his attendants to first bring a glass of milk for his assailant also, because he seemed so scared and thirsty. In this way, showing mercy and kindness towards even his mortal enemy, Ali succumbed to his injuries after two days.

(Adapted from http://www.ezsoftech.com/stories/imamali4.asp)

3. Androcles And The Lion

Once upon a time, when slavery was a very common practice in many countries, their masters treated slaves very harshly. They were made to do all kinds of hard labor day and night and were given very little food to survive. If any of the slaves tried to escape, they were soon captured by the Master's soldiers, imprisoned in dungeons, and then mercilessly killed by being thrown before hungry beasts.

Androcles was one such unfortunate slave, who tried to escape by running to a thick dense jungle. But soon he found himself facing a giant ferocious lion. Naturally Androcles was terrified to his bone, and was looking for all the possible places to hide or run, but when he looked once again at this giant lion, he saw that the lion was not making any preparations or gestures to pounce upon Androcles or devour him, instead it was trying to show its extended right paw, and looking at Androcles with sort of pitiable beseeching eyes. When Androcles looked closely at the lion's paw, he saw that there was a big thorn stuck in the paw, and blood was coming out from the wound. Androcles immediately understood, what the lion wanted, so he fearlessly went near it, and very gently pulled out the thorn. Immediately the lion felt so much relief, that it started licking Androcles's hand (to express its thanks), and soon disappeared into the jungle.

Hardly, Androcles had the time to feel good about his deed, and think about his next plan, that the king's soldiers came looking after him, and after putting him back in chains, drove him back to the city.

He was presented before the king, who ordered that Androcles should be put in a dungeon, and after one week, he should be thrown before a hungry lion. He also ordered that all the residents of the city including their slaves must watch this spectacle, so that in future no other slave should dare to escape.

So on the appointed date, all the residents of the city, along with many slaves were gathered in a public arena, and poor Androcles tightly bound in chains was made to stand in the middle of the arena, and soon a ferocious lion who had not eaten for many days was let loose on him. Naturally the hungry lion immediately ran towards poor Androcles, as if it would devour him in a single morsel, but to the amazement of all the audience, when it came close to Androcles, it immediately stopped and like a pet animal, lovingly started licking Androcles hands and feet. The entire audience, including the king was completely surprised by this strange behavior of the hungry lion. So he sent his soldiers to go and see, what was the reason. When they approached near the lion, with drawn swords, but still trembling in fear, Androcles addressed them and said: "Please do not worry, because this lion has recognized me, as the one who pulled a thorn from its paw, a few days earlier. For this act of kindness, it would not think of hurting me and it would not hurt any one in my company." So the soldiers went back to the king, and reported the entire story. Upon listening to this story, the king was very much pleased, and he ordered that both Androcles, and the lion be set free.

(Adapted from Aesop http://www.pitt.edu/~dash/type0156.html)

SERVING OTHERS:

A KIN TO THE QUALITY of loving- kindness is the quality of serving others, which has been emphasized in all the religions, I have come across, or read about, as is evident from the following few quotes.

1. "Let no one seek his own good, but the good of his neighbor." (*Christianity*. 1. Corinthians 10.24)
2. "Without selfless service, no one ever receives the fruits of their rewards. Serving others is the most excellent action." (Sikhism. SGGS p.992)
3. "Strive constantly to serve the welfare of the world; by devotion to selfless work one attains the supreme
4. goal in life. Do your work with the welfare of others in mind." (*Hinduism*. Bhagwad Gita 3.10.26) 4. The best of men are those, who are useful to others."

1. Dashrath Manjhi And The Mountain

Dashrath Manjhi was a landless farmer in India, who lived with his wife in a remote mountainous village. People living in that village had to go around a rocky mountain for hours to reach the nearest market town. So the villagers requested the government offi cials, many times, to at least cut a small path through the mountain, so that it could save them the time and trouble of trekking around the mountain, but no body listened to these poor helpless villagers.

Once Manjhi asked his wife to bring some water for him from a pond across the hill. But unluckily, her foot slipped, and she had a serious accident. It took Manjhi and his neighbors many hours to take her to the nearest hospital, and she ultimately died.

Touched by the loss of his beloved wife, Manjhi approached his neighbors to come and join him in cutting a path through the mountain, so that this kind of tragedy may not afflict others. But none of them volunteered to join him, because the task seemed so difficult and impossible. Some even ridiculed him, for thinking about such a "foolish" idea.

So then taking a hammer and chisel in his hand Manjhi started on this project all by himself. He would rise early in the morning, and start chiseling on the mountain till late in the evening, without caring for any food or water. If some passer by or village neighbor brought him something to eat or drink, he would take that, otherwise he would continue his work till the evening.

This way, he continued to chisel a cut through the mountain for almost twenty two years, and was ultimately successful in making a 360 feet long and 30 feet wide path through the hill, which was accessible by bicycle, and motorcycle.

He was later rewarded by the then chief minister of Bihar state, India. In 2016, Indian Post issued a postage stamp, featuring him. He ultimately died with a satisfaction that he lived a life of steadfast and sincere service to his neighbors for generations to come.

(Adapted from https://en.wikipediaorg/wiki/Dashrath_Manjhi)

2. How Abdu'l-Bahá Served His Enemy

'Abdu'l-Bahá was the Head of the Bahá'í Faith appointed by the Prophet-Founder, Bahá'u'lláh. There were many people who believed in existing traditions and could not tolerate the claims of a new revelation from God. Therefore they persecuted them. They had been exiled from their native Persia to the Ottoman Empire and finally to the penal colony of Akka. After the Young Turk rebellion all prisoners of conscious were freed. At that time 'Abdu'l-Bahá settled in Haifa.

Before He was freed, 'Abdu'l-Bahá had directed His followers to purchase land on Mount Carmel and begin construction on a mausoleum for the Báb, the Prophet-Herald of Bahá'u'lláh. His enemies spread rumors that the building was to be a fort for a future rebellion. Believing this, the Governor ordered 'Abdu'l-Bahá, along with his family, back to the prison. 'Abdu'l-Bahá kept teaching His Faith and living a life of service.

His enemies couldn't tolerate any such thing. They so effectively poisoned the ears of the new Governor, that he decided to take over all Bahá'ís shops and leave them no means of survival. However, before the police could come and take over the shops, 'Abdu'l-Bahá'í advised his followers not to open their shops the next morning. The police found them closed and had to return empty handed. While the Bahá'ís' shops were still closed, orders came from the central government that the Governor had been removed from office and the police were ordered to escort the Governor to Damascus.

Hearing this news, instead of feeling any joy over his enemy's banishment from the city, 'Abdu'l-Bahá'í went to the Governor and, besides advising him not to feel sad, asked him what he could do for him.

The Governor was totally surprised and could not believe his ears, hearing such kind words from the one whom he considered his worst enemy. When he was assured about the sincerity and genuineness of 'Abdu'l-Bahá's offer, he said that he would feel most obliged if he could arrange to escort his family to Damascus also.

'Abdu'l-Bahá assigned this task to one of his most trusted followers. The Governor was overjoyed on meeting his family. He wanted to richly reward the escort, and send some costly presents for 'Abdu'l-Bahá to express his thanks. The escort politely refused any reward, saying that he was only obeying his Master's orders. Then the Governor requested him to take a letter to his Master.

"Oh,'Abdu'l-Bahá," he wrote. "I pray you to pardon me. I did not understand. I did not know you. I have done you great evil. You have rewarded me with great good."

(Adapted from "Stories about Abdu'l-Bah'a", Bah'I" Publishing Trust India)

3. Gautam Buddha and the Pigeon.

Gautam Buddha, whose childhood name was Siddhartha, was the founder of Buddhism. He was born at Lumbini Nepal. His father Suddhodana was the king of the small state of Kapilwastu. His mother Maya Devi was a very pious and compassionate lady, but she died immediately after the birth of Siddhartha. So Siddhartha was raised by his aunt (the sister of Maya Devi). As was the custom in those days, his father once consulted a sage by the name Asit Muni, about the future of this young child, who after examining all the signs on the child's body, and the configuration of the stars at the time of his birth told the king that his son would either become a great king or a great holy man.

Naturally, the king Suddhodana preferred that his son should become a great king, rather than a holy man. So from the early age, he started to provide the young child, all kinds of luxuries and give him all kinds of training, so that he may grow up to be a brave warrior, and a sagacious king, and not a wandering holy man or recluse. As a precaution, he appointed personal servants for the child, who were instructed to provide him with all kinds of entertainments, but never to let him go outside the confines of the palace and see for himself, how the people in his kingdom were actually living, and struggling with their difficulties.

Prince Siddhartha, obediently carried out his father's commands, and became proficient in his studies, and marshal arts, including the use of arms, such as sword fencing, and using the bow and arrows.

But in spite of all the time spent in luxuries, entertainments, and arms training, Siddhartha, would find time to go and sit in his garden, and do meditation. In this way, he grew up to be a very kind, gentle and compassionate boy.

One day, it so happened that when Siddhartha, was sitting in his garden, all by himself, he noticed that a small beautiful pigeon fell from the sky, on to the ground, near him. He further noticed that the pigeon had been badly wounded, and was struggling for its life.

Siddhartha, immediately rushed to the aid of this wounded pigeon, called his personal servant, and the royal physician, who after cleaning the pigeon's wounds, applied the necessary ointment.

But soon, holding a bow and arrow, Siddhartha's elder brother came looking for the pigeon, and started to pick it up, saying, "This is my pigeon, I shot him down from the sky, I would enjoy its meat." But Siddhartha, did not let him get to the pigeon, saying that he won't let his brother do any such thing, because, he saved the pigeon, it belongs to him. Before the dispute could grow further, the physician said that since the pigeon was his patient, he would take it to the king, and let him decide, to whom it should be given.

So both parties went and presented their case to the king. After due deliberations with his ministers, the king decided that although, the elder son has a first claim on the pigeon, because he shot it down from the sky, yet in the final analysis, it belonged to Siddhartha, because without his timely help, it would have died. In his view the love and compassion shown by the younger brother in saving the pigeon's life is of more value than the marksmanship of the elder brother.

So Siddhartha was given full custody of the pigeon. He took care of it for some more days, and when it got fully recovered, he released it into the open, so that it could fly back to its family and friends, and enjoy their company.

(Adapted from a story the author heard in school days)

FAITH IN ONE
SUPREME POWER

N O MATTER, BY WHAT name they call, whether it is God, Lord, Allah, Bhagwan, Waheguru, almost all religions teach us to have faith in one supreme power, who is the creator of this universe, and all living beings in it. Most of the religions, further teach us to love and worship this power, and consider all human beings as our siblings, and therefore we should love them irrespective of their faith, race, or origin. Another most important thing that all religions teach us is to have complete faith in the super power that religion professes to represent, and worship only this power, and reject all others and worship no human being, or lesser god or goddess, as is illustrated by the following stories.

1. Devotee Prehlad And Demon King.

This is a very famous Hindu legend, that there once lived a king by the name of Harnakash. He somehow pleased God so much that he was granted these boons that no human being, no animal, and no natural element (such as water, air, or fire) could kill him. He was also blessed that he would neither die inside any room, nor outside, and he would not die during the day, or during night. On being granted these boons Harnakash thought that he has become immortal, and now even God cannot kill him. So he became so puffed up and arrogant, that he started behaving, as if he himself was the all- powerful God. Therefore, he issued strict command throughout his kingdom, that from now on, every body should stop worshipping God, and instead should worship him. Any body, who dared to disobey this command, would face most torturous public execution, so that no one else would dare to disobey the king's orders.

But God has His own ways to show His supremacy, and teach lessons to such self- conceited persons. So when Harnakash's own son named Prehlad was sent to school, and asked to worship Harnakash, he refused to do so, and started openly worshipping God. Seeing him, his other classmates also started doing the same thing. The teacher tried his utmost to persuade Prehlad to desist from God's worship, but he did not budge. Therefore, ultimately the teacher went to the king, and reported, how his own son refused to worship him, and worship only God, and emboldened by Prehlad's behavior, many other students had also started following his example.

Hearing this news, Harnakash's face became red with anger, and he immediately summoned Prehlad to his presence. Hearing this news, Prehlad's mother became very worried and afraid about her son's safety, so she immediately tried to intervene, and started counseling Prehlad to obey his father, and do as he wished. But Prehlad refused to waver from his faith in God, and boldly presented himself to his father.

On finding Prehlad so obstinate, Harnakash gave orders to shut him down in a dark room, and not to give him any food or water, till he pleads for mercy, and starts to worship Harnakash. But even after many days in the dark dungeon, Prehlad did not make any call for mercy, and he kept praying to God. When Harnaakash found that the imprisonment did not have any effect on Prehlad's resolve, he ordered that he should be thrown from a high mountain. But when this punishment was carried out, nothing happened to Prehlad, because a tree on the hill slope miraculously saved him. Harnakash tried many other ways to get Prehlad killed, but every time, somehow or other God kept saving him.

Infuriated at all these failed attempts, Harnakash finally took out his own sword, and with a rage proceeded towards Prehlad saying: "let me see, how your God saves you now? But right at this moment, a strange entity, which was half lion, and half human came out of a pillar, and gripping him in his paws, said in a roaring voice: " O' Harnakash, here I have come to save my devotee, who kept his faith in me, and without going back on any of my boons given to you, I am going to end your reign of terror. Now see for yourself, that I am neither an animal, nor a human being, and it is dusk so it is neither day, nor night, and here placing you half inside the room, and outside, I am going to kill you with my teeth and sharp paws."

Harnakash tried to plead for mercy, but it was too late now, and thus because of his unflinching faith Prehlad was saved, and his story would continue to inspire others to never waver in their faith and trust in God.

(Adapted from a hymnal story in Sri Guru Granth Sahib)

2. Faith And The Fiery Furnace

Written by Daniel* in Daniel 3:1-30

Once upon a time, when king Nebuchadnezzar was ruling over Babylon, he installed a huge gold statue to celebrate his victory in a recent war. He issued strict orders that from now on all his citizens must worship this idol daily, by playing many musical instruments, such as horns, flutes, harps, lyres, and psaltery. He further ordered that as soon as the citizens hear the sounds of these instruments being played in a symphony, they must all bend down and start worshipping this idol. He commanded that anybody, who dared to ignore or disobey this command, should be thrown in a fiery furnace.

A few days after, the issuing of this order, the king was informed by one of his soldiers, that all citizens of his empire were regularly obeying his command, and bending down in worship of his golden idol, as soon as they heard the sound of symphony. But all except three jews named Shadrach, Meshach, and Abed-Nego did not obey his command.

Hearing this news, he immediately commanded that these three Jews be arrested, and produced before him. When bound in chains these Jews were presented before the king, in a thundering voice, he said: "O Jews, is it true that you have knowingly, and willingly disobeyed my command, and have refused to pray and worship this gold idol of mine?" All three of them, boldly replied: "O' mighty king, we do respect your commands, and faithfully obey them, but our faith prohibits us from worshipping any god, goddess, or idol, except the one supreme God, who is the creator of this universe."

Hearing this reply the king said: " I don't know, what God you are talking about, I do not see him anywhere, therefore, you better worship and pray before this gold idol, as all other citizens of my empire are doing, otherwise, I would order that, all three of you should be thrown into this burning fiery furnace, and I would see, which God of yours, saves you from being burnt to death in a few seconds."

When the king saw that even this command of his did not scare the Jews, and they remained steadfast in their faith in the one supreme God, he ordered that all these three men should be tightly bound together in chains, and thrown into the fiery furnace, which should be heated seven times more than the usual.

The king's guards immediately started to carry out his commands. They heated the furnace with extra fuel, and when it was heated to the highest degree possible, they bound the three Jews in strong iron chains, and threw them in the furnace. But it so happened that when the guards started to look down into the furnace, a big flame of fire leapt towards them, and burnt them to the ashes.

After waiting for a few minutes, the king and his companions climbed a nearby high place, from where they could safely look into the furnace. To their amazement they saw that all those three Jews, along with another ghostlike figure were walking in the furnace, as if nothing had happened. Then the king realized that it must be God Himself, or His special angel, who had saved them.

So he went near the furnace, and asked them to come out, and proclaimed that from now on all his citizens should worship no one except the one Almighty God.

(Adapted from Holy Bible Daniel 3:1-30)

3. A Little Girl's Firm Faith In God

Once, there was a king named Duni Chand, who used to rule over a large area, near modern day Amritsar in Punjab, India. The king Duni Chand had seven daughters, he loved them all, and used to provide them with all kinds of comforts, and provisions for their enjoyment.

One day all the seven sisters were sitting together and talking about, how good their father was. At one point, all the girls except the youngest girl Rajni, said, that they really depended so much on their father, that if he were not to support them, or take care of them, they might have nothing to eat, or wear. But Rajni kept silent. So when asked for her silence, Rajni replied, that no doubt their father loved them very much, and provided them with whatever they need, yet ultimately it is God, who is the real provider and protector of all creatures, and even if their father stopped taking care of them, if God so wills, He would make some alternative arrangements for their care.

One of the sisters reported these remarks of Rajni to the king. Upon hearing this thing, the king, became very mad, and assumed that this girl of his was very ungrateful. Therefore, in order to teach her a lesson, he found out a completely handicapped leper, married young Rajni to him, and kicking both of them out of his palace, said to her: " Let me see now, how your God provides for you, and your cripple husband?

Without making any fuss, poor Rajni arranged to put her husband in a hand pulled small wooden cart, and started going from place to place, looking for some menial job, which could provide them with their daily food. While going on their search, she reached near a small pool, which was surrounded by small trees. She left her husband under a tree near the pool, and went to the nearby village, in order to earn some food.

When after a long time, Rajni came back; she noticed that instead of her handicapped leper husband, a tall dark hale and healthy man was sitting in his place. She asked, him who he was. The man replied that he was her husband. At this point, Rajni started to make a noise, that this man was an imposter, and some how had hidden or killed her real husband, and now wanted to take advantage of her youth. Hearing the noise, many people from the village came down, and took both Rajni and this man, who claimed to be her husband, to Guru Ji, for adjudication. First, Rajni told her story, that how while talking with her sisters; she had expressed her view, that in reality God is the provider and sustainer of all of us, and not even our parents. Hearing this remark, her father became very mad, because he thought that, it was he, and not God, who took care of his family and his people. Therefore in order to teach her a lesson, he married Rajni to a handicapped leper, and challenged her to show him, who would take care of her and her husband. Then he asked the young man, who claimed to be her husband, to tell his story.

The young man narrated the following incident. He said: "When Rajni was gone, and I was just looking around, waiting for my wife to come back, I noticed a very strange thing happening. First I could not believe my eyes. But then after making sure that I was not dreaming, I saw, that there were some black crows sitting on the tree above me. One by one, they would dive into the pool near me, and then fly out as white swans. I thought, that this pool, must have some magical qualities, so some how, I dragged myself out of my box cart, and crawled to the pool, and while holding on to a small plant, I managed to take a dip in the pool, and when I came out, I found out that all my leprosy signs were gone, and I could move around like a normal healthy young man. But as a proof, that I am the same leper, who was married to Rajni, I want to show, you this hand of mine, which I had to keep outside, holding the plant, and which is still afflicted with leprosy, and cannot function, like the other hand."

Hearing this story, Guru Ji told that this young man is truly Rajni's husband, and not an imposter. God has done this miracle to prove the truth of the firm faith of Rajni in God. Hearing this news, Rajni's father, also came there to confess his fault, and took Rajni and her husband back to his palace, and accorded them due respect, and honor.

Since then this place is considered very sacred. This pool is now a part of the huge tank, around Harimander Sahib (Golden Temple, Amritsar, India), and the tree under which Rajni's husband sat is known as Dukh Bhanjani Beri (meaning the pain destroying tree), and people from far and wide come to take a dip in the tank near the tree.

(Adapted from a tale in the Sikh legends).

HUMILITY, AND ACCEPTANCE OF GOD'S WILL

BESIDES THE ABOVE QUALITIES, all faiths try to teach us to be always humble, and accept God's will in all circumstances, no matter how unfavorable or unpleasant these circumstances may be, as is evident from the following quotes and stories:

1. Blessed are the meek, for they shall inherit the earth. (Christianity. Mathew 5.5)
2. Successful indeed are the believers, who are humble in their prayers------. (Islam. Quran 23.1-5)
3. Be humble, be harmless, Have no pretension. (Hinduism. Bhagwad Gita 13.7-8)

4. Without merit am I; all merit is Thine. Thine Lord are all merits-by what tongue have I power to praise Thee. (Sikhism, Adi Granth, Wadhans, M: 5 p.577)

5. Be of an exceedingly humble spirit, for the end of man is the worm. (Judaism. Mishnah, Abot 4.4)

1. Guru Amar Dass Ji And His Rival

Guru Amar Dass Ji is the third Guru Of Sikhs. Before being anointed as Guru, he was known as Bhai Amar Dass, and he used to worship the goddess Vaishnav Devi, and used to lead pilgrimage parties to her temple. But in spite of living like this and spending many years in such rituals, his mind still felt restless. One day, by chance, he happened to listen to a sweet shabad (hymn) being sung by Amro (his nephew's wife). He was so moved by the divine message of this hymn, that he immediately went and begged Amro to tell him, who was this divine soul, whose message she was reciting. She replied that she was reciting one of the hymns of the first Sikh Guru Nanak Dev Ji, who has now departed to his heavenly abode, and now her father Guru Angad Dev Ji is providing spiritual guidance to his followers. Hearing this reply, Amar Dass Ji requested her to immediately take him to his father, and the very next day both of them proceeded to Goindwal to see Guru Angad Dev Ji. Being mesmerized by his very first sight, Amar Dass Ji fell down at Guru Angad Dev Ji's feet, and begged him to accept him as his disciple, and assign him the most menial task of his household. So Guru Angad Dev Ji assigned him the duty of daily going on foot to the near by river and bring water for his early morning bath.

Amar Dass Ji, who was about 60 years of age at that time faithfully carried out this service for full twelve years, without missing a single day, no matter, whether it was stormy, rainy, or there was a strong wind. Once, it so happened, that while it was still dark, he was carrying a pitcher full of water on his head, his foot tripped over a wooden peg, driven by a weaver, and he fell down, but did not let the water pitcher fall from his head. Upon hearing the noise, the weaver and his wife shouted some very insulting remarks against Amar Dass Ji.

When Guru Angad Dev Ji heard about this incident, and how in spite of his old age (72 years), did not let the water for his Guru fall down, he was so pleased that ignoring his own two sons, he anointed Amar Dass Ji as the next Guru, and he himself departed for his heavenly abode.

Guru Angad Dev Ji's sons particularly Daattu did not like that Amar Dass, who was just their menial servant, should become the next Guru, and they should be totally ignored like this. So one day, when sitting on a raised dais, Guru Amar Dass Ji was addressing his congregation, Daattu angrily entered the room, went straight to the dais, and kicking Guru Amar Dass Ji on the butt, shouted: "This seat of Guru ship belongs to us, you are a mere servant of our household, and you better go away from here."

Seeing this kind of insult to their Guru, many of the Sikhs got enraged, and rushed to give a severe beating to Daattu. But before they could do any such thing, Guru Amar Dass Ji quickly sat down on the floor, and catching hold of Daattu's feet, most humbly addressed him and said: "O the respected son of my Guru, you are so young, and your bones are still so delicate and soft, but with age, my bones might have become too hard, and might have hurt your poor delicate bones. Please let me massage your feet, so that your pain may become a little less. As per your orders, I am right away going away from here back to my ancestral place in Basarke.

So Guru Ji immediately went out of the room, rode back to his house in Basarke, closed himself in a room, and put a note on the entrance door, that any one who tries to enter, would be severely cursed.

But in spite of Daattu's efforts, the Sikhs, refused to accept him as their Guru. They soon found out about the whereabouts of Guru Amar Das Ji, and making a big hole in the back wall, entered Guru Ji's room, and re installed him as their true Guru.

(Adapted from a story in Sikh history)

2. Prophet Mohammad And An Arrogant Woman.

Prophet Mohammad was in the habit of daily going to the mosque for prayers. There was only one road, which led from his house to the mosque. So he had to traverse this road every day, both while coming and going. It so happened that along the road there were many houses. In one of those houses on the upper floor used to live a woman, who was in the habit of sweeping her floor about the same time, when Mohammad was passing beneath her house. It is not known, whether this woman had any grudge against the prophet, or she did not have any manners, but what she used to do was that as soon as she was done sweeping, she would collect all the trash in a small pan and throw it out of her upper floor window, making sure that it fell down on the prophet, and would keep standing in the window to see how the prophet responded to such an insult. But to her disappointment, the prophet would simply dust off the droppings, show a smile on his face, and would proceed on his way to the mosque.

Seeing this response from the prophet, the woman would become all the more determined to insult him the next day, even with much more trash. The woman tried many days, but she could not get any response, not even a single angry word or gesture from the prophet.

But one day, as usual when the prophet was passing below the window of this lady, no trash came down from there. The prophet was so used to this thing, that he stood waiting for the trash, thinking, that may be the lady might have become a little late. But when even after waiting for a long time, no trash fell down on him, the prophet became worried, and without caring for the disparaging comments of the neighbors, he climbed the stairs leading to that woman's upper floor apartment, and knocked on her door.

When the woman came out, and saw that it is the same man, on whom she daily throws her trash, she became very terrified, and was about to say some words in apology, when the prophet Mohammad, humbly said: " O' my respected lady, you don't need to have any fear that I have come to scold you or harm you in any way, but I have to enquire, why you did not honor me with your "blessings" today. Are you O. K and not suffering from any illness or trouble? If yes, please let this servant know, so that he may be of some service to you, and you may soon recover your complete health, and resume blessing me with your trash like before."

Hearing those most humble sweet words, the woman was moved to tears, and begged him to pardon her.

(Adapted from an incident narrated by A.S.Alloo in Bilal's Bed Time Stories website "Al-Islam.org")

3. A King and His Wise Minister

Once upon a time, there was a very popular king, who had a very capable and efficient council of ministers to always guide him. Among his council of ministers, was a very god loving and wise minister, who truly believed that whatever God does is for our best, therefore no matter, what happens, weather seemingly good or bad, we should always readily accept every happening in our life as God's will, and be always thankful to God for any incident in our life. Therefore, whenever the king was discussing any new incident or happening in his kingdom or even a sickness in his family, this wise minister would remark: "Let us thank God for this."

One time the king developed a serious boil on one of his fingers, and in spite of many efforts to cure, it worsened so much, that ultimately this finger had to be amputated. One day, when the king was sharing his grief over the loss of his finger with his council of ministers, and all were expressing their concern and sympathy, this wise minister remarked:"

Let us thank God for this favor on our great king." Hearing this remark, naturally the king got very much mad at him, and immediately ordered that this minister should be put in the darkest dungeon, and let us see if he still keeps saying: "Let us thank God for this favor."

With the passage of time the king got used to having one less finger on his hand, and resumed his normal activities and past times, including hunting.

In one of his hunting expeditions, the king lost his way, and got separated from his companions, and was caught by a gang of dacoits, who were returning to their hideout, after a very successful robbery in the nearby city. Before starting on this adventure, they had pledged to their goddess, that they would sacrifice a full grown, hale and hearty human being, if their robbery mission was successfully accomplished.

So, when they saw the king, who was in ordinary hunting attire, lonely loitering, they caught hold of him, securely bound him with ropes, and took him to the goddess's temple. But, when they placed him on the sacrifice platform, and were inspecting to make sure, he was securely bound, and when lit on fire, he would not be able to move or jump out of the platform, they noticed that one of his fingers was missing. The chief of the dacoits, who was very much superstitious, and a stickler for details, ordered that this man was no good for their sacrifice. Therefore, they let him lose, and decided to look for another suitable victim for their sacrifice.

The king was very much pleasantly surprised at this development, and as soon as he was able to find his way to his palace, he immediately went to the dungeon, where his wise minister was imprisoned. After releasing him, the king said: O' my wise and faithful minister, you were right. As suggested by you, I should have been thankful to God, for the loss of my finger. I am very sorry, that instead of listening to your advice, I threw you in this dungeon, and made you suffer through such tortures."

Upon listening this, the minister replied: " No your highness, you need not apologize for any thing. I believe that my imprisonment was also a God's favor upon me, and I am extremely thankful to Him for this."

Hearing this reply, the king was completely amazed, and asked, how could that be a God's favor to you?" The minister replied: " Your majesty, if I were not in prison, I would have accompanied you on your hunting trip, and unlike others, I would have never forsaken you, when you lost your way. Then naturally, I would also have been captured by the dacoits along with you, and being a complete person, with all my limbs intact, they would have sacrificed me, instead of you."

(Adapted from similar stories recorded on the Internet sites of many faiths).

4. Imam Husain And His Maid

Imam Husain was one of two sons of Ali, the son- in- law of prophet Mohammad, and fourth Khalifa of Islam. Once Husain's maid slave unwittingly dropped hot soup on her Master. Naturally, she was very scared that now her Master is going to severely punish her.

But, before Husain could open his mouth and say anything, she immediately, started to recite a quote from the Quran, which says: " Those who control their Anger---"

Upon hearing these few words, Husain smiled and said: "I am not angry."

Then the maid started to recite the next part of this quote, and said: "----And are forgiving towards people----".

Husain responded and said: "I have already forgiven you."

The wise maid then completed the quote, and said: "----Allah loves those, who do good-----".

Husain was so much pleased with this wise maid that he set her free.

(Adapted from Holy Quran, Surah Aal-e-Imran (3), verse 134)

5. The Story Of Job

Once upon a time in the land of Uz, lived a man by the name of Job. He was a very righteous person, always kind and merciful to the poor and the needy, and stayed away from any kinds of evil habits, such as lust, anger, greed, or slander.

He was blessed with abundant wealth, and possessions in the form of many houses, and hundreds of cattle, camels, land holdings, and many servants. He was also blessed with seven obedient sons, and three loving daughters.

One day, while discussing the behavior of men on earth, God said to Satan, that his servant Job was very upright, and blameless person, and very much reveres Him. But Satan replied that Job's uprightness, and respect for God, was only due to the fact that God had blessed him with all kinds of riches, and pleasures of family, and happiness. The real test of his virtues and faithfulness would come, if all his possessions, wealth, and family, were taken away from him. God accepted Satan's challenge, and allowed him to take away from Job, what he wanted, except his life.

So one day, when all Job's sons and daughters were eating and drinking at the house of the eldest son, a messenger came to Job, and told him that a large gang of dacoits suddenly came, killed all the servants, and stole away all their cattle. While he was telling this story, another servant came and told that suddenly a tornado came, uprooted the house in which all his sons and daughters were eating and drinking, and killed them all. Even after hearing such tragic news one after the other, Job did not lose his balance of mind, but quietly rose, tore open his shirt, and bowed down in prayer, and said: "God gave, and God has taken away, blessed is God's Name."

Observing this attitude of Job of happily accepting God's will, and to test him further, Satan obtains the permission of God to afflict Job's body with boils, and is made to sit in ashes. Seeing this pitiable condition, Job's wife asks him to curse God and die. But Job is still not sure, what to do, and he asks his wife: " I wonder if cursing God would bring us any good, I fear we may receive even more evil."

Then job laments the day, he was born, and wishes to die, but even this wish of his is denied. So while living in this abject condition and misery, three of his friends, Eliphaz, Bildad, and Zophar, come to console him. Job contrasts his previous fortune, with his present miserable plight. His friends suggest that his present suffering might be due to some sin he might have committed. To this Job responds, that throughout his life he has not committed any evil act, and he has always stayed away from evil ways, and has always tried to remain righteous, compassionate, and benevolent to the poor and needy, and a just God would not treat him so harshly and He should not make his creatures, suffer so miserably.

Then another younger friend Elihu comes to console Job, and offer some words of wisdom to him, but that doesn't satisfy Job. While this dialogue was still going on, God speaks from a whirlwind, and challenges Job's wisdom, and asks Job to answer such questions, as where was he, when He (God) laid the foundation of the earth, or the limits of the sea and what does he know, when the wild mountain goats bear the young, or when the deer give birth?

Finding himself unable to answer any of God's questions, Job acknowledged his complete ignorance in all such matters, and confessed his folly in blaming God for any of his misfortunes, and said: "I abhor myself and repent in dust and ashes."

Hearing these words of humility, and repentance, God became merciful, and blessed Job with double of his previous wealth and possessions, and he lived happily for one hundred and forty more years with many of his generations.

(Adapted from the book of Job in The Holy Bible)

SELFISH DESIRE, LUST, ANGER, GREED, EGO, AND SLANDER

BESIDE TEACHING US THE positive values, such as truth, love, compassion, and forgiveness, different religions admonish us against some negative traits, such as selfish desire, lust, anger, greed, ego, and slander, as is evident from the following quotes and stories:

1. There are three gates to self- destructive hell. These are lust, anger, and greed. (*Hinduism*. Bhagwad Gita 16.21)

2. In desire is man born, from desire he consumes objects of various tastes. By desire is he led away bound, buffered across the face. Bound by evil qualities he is

chastised. (*Sikhism*. Adi Granth, Sri Raga Ashtpadi M: 1, p. 61)

3. What causes wars, and what causes fighting among you? Is it not your passions that are at war in your members? You desire, and do not have; so you kill. And you covet and cannot obtain; so you fight and wage war. (*Christianity*. James 4.1.3)

4. The man who gathers flowers (of sensual pleasure), whose mind is distracted and who is insatiate in desires, the Destroyer brings under his sway. (*Buddhism*. Dhammpada 48)

5. There is no crime greater than having too many desires: There is no disaster greater than not being content: There is no misfortune greater than being covetous. (*Taoism*. Tao Te Chang 46)

6. Have you seen him who makes his desire his god, and God sends him astray purposely, and seals up his hearing and his heart, and sets on his sight a covering? Who will lead him after God (has condemned him)? Will you not then heed? (*Islam*. Qur'an 45.23)

1. Punishment To god Indira For his Lust:

Beside one God, the Hindu mythology talks about many gods and goddesses. Among them god Indira is considered the king of all gods, and is believed to be the one who is in charge of clouds and rains. It is also believed that this god has a very extensive and luxurious court in which many very beautiful dancers or fairies keep dancing. But in spite of all these luxuries, god Indira's lust is never satisfied. So he is always on the look out for more and more beautiful girls.

One day his eyes fell on a very beautiful girl, who was the wife of a sage named Gautam. So Indira started to make plans to seduce her. For this purpose, he started to stalk her husband and notice his habits, such as his daily routine. He found out that early in the morning when a rooster crows, the sage wakes up and goes to the nearby river, and comes back only after doing his ablution and morning prayers.

So Indira decided that this would be his best chance to take advantage of the sage's absence. Therefore one night he went and hid behind a bush and started waiting for the crowing of the rooster. But as is often the case in such situations, he could not wait till the morning and the rooster's crowing, so he himself emitted a voice like that of a rooster, with the result that the sage Gautam thought it to be the sign of morning, and he proceeded to the river to take his bath and do the morning prayers.

So after a few minutes, Indira disguised as sage Gautam entered the house. Gautama's wife was surprised by her husband's early return, but being a good simple woman thought, that her husband might have forgotten something, and asked Indira, about it. But Indira said to her, "Today I want to make love to you before taking my bath." Saying this he immediately proceeded to satisfy his sexual desire. In the mean time sage Gautam intuitively guessed that there was something wrong, so he quickly returned to his house. But when he entered his house, he found Indira, and his wife in a compromising position. He was naturally very much enraged at this horrible crime of god Indira, and cursed him that he would have thousand vulva marks on his body, which would never be erased, and he would live in shame and dishonor forever.

(Adapted from Hindu legends mentioned in Sikh holy scripture Sri Guru Granth Sahib)

2. Devotee Nam Dev And Proud Priests

Nam Dev was a poor low caste Hindu, who used to feed himself and his family by dyeing and manually printing the clothes of his neighbors. He used to live in a small hut in village Pandarpur in Maharashtar (India). In spite of his poverty and low social status in the society, he so loved God that he used to always remain contented and kept remembering God even while doing his job and doing other chores.

Once while on his way to a client's house, for an urgent appointment, he happened to pass nearby Hindu temple, where some Pundits were doing their ritual worship. Nam Dev also felt a strong urge to join them and pay homage to the deity. But, as he was in a hurry, instead of going to the special place for depositing his shoes, he tucked the shoes under his belt, quickly ran towards the temple and entered the main gate, and fervently joined the Pundits in reciting the mantras which they were chanting.

At first all other participants were very much impressed by the zeal and devotion of this new worshipper, but then some of the pundits recognized him as the low caste calico printer, who was even carrying his shoes on his body. So immediately those pundits caught hold of Namdev, and angrily asked him, how he a low caste printer dared to enter their holy temple, and that too while carrying his shoes on his body, and started beating and kicking him.

Nam Dev very humbly tried to explain that he was in a hurry, and could not afford to lose his shoes, but the egoistic pundits, did not heed any of his pleas, and kicked him out of the temple.

Poor Nam Dev went and sat at the back of the temple, shedding tears and feeling so sad and depressed about this kind of treatment at the hands of those self- conceited pundits. Then he even started talking to God, in his mind, and asking Him, why would He allow such an insult of His devotee, which in reality is insult of God Himself? Then as if God answered him, by saying that, he should not mind this disgrace, and he would be rewarded later with salvation. But Nam Dev was not satisfied with this answer, he said to God, that this salvation upon death would do no good, as no body would know about it. Therefore, if God really wanted to restore the honor of His devotee, He should do something right now, which is visible to every body. Upon hearing this request, God immediately so turned the entire sanctuary that its face was towards Nam Dev, and its back towards the egoistic pundits.

When those pundits and other people, who had so badly beaten and kicked poor Nam Dev, noticed this change, they immediately realized their terrible mistake, and fell down at the feet of Nam Dev, begging for his forgiveness.

(Adapted from a hymn in Sikh holy scripture Sri Guru Granth Sahib))

3. Four Selfish and Greedy Friends

Once there lived four poor friends in a city. One day, they decided to go hiking in a nearby wooded area. While passing through a field, they noticed that the ground near a stone was unusually high, and unlike the surrounding area, without any grass. Their curiosity led them to believe that this place was recently dug, and filled again, after burying something in it. So they started digging that place up, and soon discovered that they were right, because in that place was buried a very big and heavy box, filled with gold coins. They were very much thrilled and delighted to find this treasure, and decided that they would divide this wealth equally among them.

But since they were very tired from walking so far, and digging, and were also hungry, they decided that two of them would go to the city to bring some food and drinks, and other two would keep sitting there, and guarding the treasure.

However soon the evil passions of selfishness, and greed overpowered their feelings of friendship, and honesty, so both parties started thinking about the ways to have this treasure all to themselves. So the party, which was supposed to go to the city, and bring food, decided to eat their food at the shop itself, and laced the food for the other two friends with deadly poison. On the other hand, the party entrusted with guarding the treasure, got their digging tools sharpened, and as soon as the friends with the foods came, they attacked them with those sharpened tools, and killed them at the spot. Then they started to eat their food, with relish, while each thinking, how could he kill the other, and have the entire treasure himself. But they did not know, that the food was laced with poison, and both became heaps of dust, before the food was even half finished. Thus because of their greed and selfishness, they not only were deprived of their hard found wealth, but their lives as well.

(Adapted from https:////www.realsikhism.com/index.php?subaction=showfull &id=1193029371&ucat=9)

4. Traders Of Seriva

Once upon a time, there lived two traveling salesmen in the kingdom of Seriva, who used to sell almost similar things. Both of them used to travel together to different towns, but in order to avoid competing with each other they used to divide the towns into two almost equal parts for selling their wares. After completing the first round, the merchants would switch their territories, and each one would go and try his luck in the part, the other had covered.

It so happened that in that city lived an old woman and her grand daughter, who although belonged to a very rich family, yet were living in very poor conditions, because of heavy business losses and the sudden deaths of their earning members. One day, when the young child was playing in the street, one of the travelling traders passed through the street, hawking his wares and displaying the same to the interested persons. When he was thus showing his wares to a neighbor, this poor little girl was also looking at them, and she took fancy to a small artificial pearl necklace, and ran to her grandmother for getting the needed money.

But when her grandmother told her that she doesn't have any money, but may be the merchant might agree to accept one of her metal pots or pans in exchange. So she took out one small pot, which although was covered with grease and soot, for not being used for many years, yet was otherwise in good shape, with no kinks, or bends. When she presented the same to the merchant, he started examining it carefully, and started to remove the soot and grease, he noticed that this pot was actually made of gold, and was very costly. But instead of offering the fair price for this gold pot, he thought of a clever idea to get this pot almost free. So looking angrily at the old woman, he said to her: "This is an old dirty pot, and of no use to me, just to please the child I can give may be a small candy, or some small trinket, but not this beautiful necklace. But the little girl just wanted that necklace, so the merchant returned the pot to the old lady, and proceeded further on his round, with the idea that in the evening, he would come back, and by then the old lady and the little girl would become agreeable to exchange that pot, for a small trinket.

After completing their respective rounds, the merchants switched their routes. When the other merchant passed through the same street in which the poor old lady, and her grand daughter lived, he was also presented with that pot. So he scrapped off some of the dust and the soot from the pot, and soon determined that the pot was actually made of solid gold, he said to the old lady: " O' madam, this pot is quite costly, may be $ 1000, because it is made of pure gold, and I can pay you only $ 500, plus the beautiful pearl necklace, your grand daughter wants. After some hesitation, the old lady accepted the offer, because she knew that it was very difficult for her to go to the city and find an honest jeweler. Soon after that the other merchant also came to try to get the pot, but was very disappointed, when he found that the other merchant, had already bought it for half price so now, he could not do any thing except to repent for his greed.

(http://www.accesstoinsight.org/lib/authors/kawasaki/ bl135.html#jat003)

5. Boy, Who Could Not Control His Anger

once upon a time there was a boy named Ahmed, who was the only son of his parents. Being the only child, he was very dear to his parents. He was overall a very good boy, being tidy, and good in his studies, but he had one major problem. He had a very terrible temper. He would start shouting and cursing at the smallest excuse, and would not even care, whether he was shouting at younger children or his elders and teachers. Naturally this made him, very unpopular with his acquaintances, and fellow students, who nicknamed him Mr. Anger. His parents advised him many times to control his temper, but he would reply that in spite of his best intentions, he was finding it impossible to control his anger. Whenever any body annoyed him, he would fly into a rage and before he could realize his mistake, he might have already shouted many curses, or tried to physically harm the other person.

Ultimately his father came up with a plan. He gave the boy a big bag of nails, and told him that next time, he felt provoked, or angry at any thing, instead of shouting, or kicking, he should take one nail out of this bag and drive it as hard and as deep, as he felt angry into a post in the fence in their backyard, and report back to him after a month. The boy agreed, so whenever he felt annoyed or mad at any person or a thing, he would go to that post in the fence, and would drive a nail in it. At first the boy got agitated so many times in a day, that he would end up pounding in almost two dozen nails in a day. But soon the boy started feeling exhausted and tired driving these nails, so he started keeping control of his temper, and the number of nails driven in the fence started decreasing. After a couple of weeks, he noted that, he had not driven even a single nail, for many days. So, after a month, he went back to his father, and told him about his progress. The father asked him to take out as many nails, as he could easily take out. The boy did exactly that.

Then the father accompanied the boy to the post, and said to the boy:" Look Ahmed, you see that even though you have taken out many nails, there are some nails which are still stuck in this post, and there are many holes and scratches in the post, where you removed the nails. Similarly angry and harsh words, shouted at somebody are like driving nails into the hearts of that person. Some words, you could retract, and apologize for, and the person concerned, may even accept your apology, but still the bad memory of those harsh words won't go away. But there are some words, and curses, which go so deep in a victim's mind, that no matter what apology you may offer the injured person is not able to forget and forgive, and he or she may try to harm you, or at least, you may lose his or her friendship or good will for you. So, next time, you feel provoked or annoyed, remember to control your temper, and do not utter any harsh words, lest you have to repent for the rest of your life."

(Adapted from http://www.ezsoftech.com/stories/ anger.management.stories. in.islam.asp)

6. The King, Who Was Proud Of His Generosity

As heard in my teens years; once upon a time, there was a king, who was so generous that he became too proud of his generosity, and used to boast, that no matter, when any body approaches him and asks for any donation, he or she will not go empty handed. But once on a hunting trip, the king was in his horse stable in a jungle, when a hungry saint visits him. Saint pleads for a donation from the king to which the latter replies that he has nothing to offer the saint in a horse stable. Saint insists and says: 'O bountiful king, you always claim that no matter, when and where, any body asks you for any donation or charity, he or she never returns empty handed. So please give me whatever you can'. Out of his misguided pride and ego, the king puts a handful of horse dung in saint's platter. Saint accepts it, blesses him and walks away quietly.

Several years later, the king returns to the same jungle on another hunting excursion. To his astonishment, he notices heaps of horse dung all over. He started to wonder; how all that horse dung got there, while there are no horses or stables around. He then noticed a small hut where the same saint whom He had met many years ago was meditating.

After paying salutations to the saint, the king enquires about the horse dung. Saint replies, 'O mighty king, if you would recall, I had visited you many years ago asking for a donation and you had given me a handful of horse dung in offering, this is your offering, that is growing bigger and bigger, which you would have to eat one day.

King is taken aback by saint's reply; in all humility, with grave repentance and melancholy, he prays to the saint and asks for redemption and solution to end the heaps of horse dung. Saint suggests that 'if people vilify you, condemn you, then this dung would disappear or else you will have to eat it'.

Upon returning to his Kingdom, he started abusing, torturing people, and roaming around drunk, which eventually led to his defamation and widespread vilification. He again returned to the saint and noticed that all the dung was gone except the amount he had originally offered to the Saint. King pleads to the Saint for settlement of that also, but the saint replies, 'there is one such godly woman in your kingdom who has not spoken against you'.

King goes to her door also. Opening the door, the woman boldly confronted the king and told him upfront that she was not the one who is going to eat his share of dung.

Heartbroken with repentance and realization the king returned to the saint and again confessed and apologized for his wrongdoing. He had to eat his share of dung, and learnt a lesson, that no matter what, one should never be too proud of oneself on any account, and should never engage in vilifying others.

(Contributed by Dr. Amarjit Singh, M.D, Rochester, Minnesota).

7. The Sage, Deer, And Hunter

Once a holy man was going to see God. On his way through a jungle, he first met a sage, and told him that he is going to see God, and asked him, if he has any question, which he wanted to ask God. With a great pride and arrogance, the sage asked him to convey this message to God that he has been sitting at this one place doing penance and worship for the last 20 years. He knows that God has previously given seats in heaven even to those devotees, who have worshipped Him for only a few months. But, he has been worshipping Him and doing hard penance for many years, so he would like to know, what special seat or place, God has reserved for Him in heaven. The man said, he would convey his message to God, and would tell him, God's response on his way back.

Next that man happened to meet a hunter, who was trying to shoot some birds with his bow and arrow. He asked the hunter the same question, that he was on his way to meet God, and if he has any question for God. The hunter very humbly replied: " O holy man, what kind of question, a sinner like me could ask God. But if you can do this favor to me, then tell God, that I know that I am a sinner, I kill poor birds, to sell their meat, and thus feed my children. I know, this is a sin, but I don't know any other way to provide for my family. So could you ask God, that I know that for a sinner like me, heaven is out of question, but would there be any place in hell for me?" Hearing this reply, the man said to the hunter that he would convey his message to God, and would tell him, God's answer on his way back.

Next, that holy person met a deer, and he asked it the same question, he had asked the sage and the hunter. The deer said: "O holy man, if you must ask, then tell God that in this area, where I live, there has been no rain for the last 12 years. With the result that most of the rivers, lakes, and ponds have gone dry, and I have to go to far off places in search of a few drops of water to drink. Many days, I have to remain thirsty and hungry. So please could you ask Him, when the rain might come? The holy man assured the deer that he would definitely convey its message to God, and would tell, what God had to say in this regard, and he proceeded further on his way.

After a few days the man returned to that jungle, and first went to meet the sage. The sage again haughtily addressed the holy man and said: "Yes, tell me, what special kind of heaven, God has built for me."

The holy man replied: " O dear sage, I am sorry to say, that upon hearing your message, instead of becoming happy, God became very angry, and said that, no matter, how long any person has worshipped Him, or what kind of penance, any body has done, He doesn't like any egoistic or arrogant person, so what to speak of any special heaven, He is not going to give him any place in ordinary hell, He was going to send him in a place, which is many times hotter, and much more torturous than ordinary hell."

After conveying this response the holy man proceeded further on his return journey, and met the bird hunter. The hunter again humbly asked him, about God's response. The holy man said to him: "O hunter, upon hearing your tale, God said, no doubt the hunter is committing grave sins by killing poor small birds, but I am always sympathetic to those persons, who humbly acknowledge their guilt, and are willing to make amends in future. Therefore, go and tell the hunter that he can still catch the birds, but instead of killing them for meat, he should sell them as house pets. If he follows this advice, all his previous sins would be pardoned, and he would be favorably considered for a place in heaven." Hearing this response the hunter was very much pleased and profusely thanked God for such a wonderful advice, which would not only save him from further sins, but could bring him much more income, because he could sell each bird as a pet at a much higher price than a few ounces of its meat.

Finally, the holy man went to see the deer, and said: "O deer, I don't have a very good news for you. I don't know, in what mood God was sitting, when I conveyed your message to Him, He very curtly replied: "Go and tell that deer, that if it has not rained for the last 12 years, it won't rain for next 12 years more." Before I could plead any more on your behalf, He waved His Hand, signaling that He didn't want to be disturbed any further. So I am sorry, I don't have any good news for you."

Hearing this reply, instead of feeling dejected or disappointed, the deer started jumping in joy, and making merry.

Watching this strange behavior of the deer, the holy man was very much surprised, and said to the deer: "I am really surprised at your strange behavior. I am feeling so sorry for you, that you would have to live without rain for another 12 years, but you are jumping in joy, as if I have brought you, such a good news that you cannot restrain yourself from dancing."

In response, the deer said: " O my dear holy man, you need to look on the bright side of this news. If God has said that there would be no rain for another 12 years, it means that it would rain after 12 years. So if I have survived for 12 years without rain, I can certainly survive another 12 years.

Is not that, a good news? And saying this the deer resumed its dancing and merry making.

Upon watching this positive attitude of the deer, and cheerfully obeying and accepting God's will, God was so much pleased that He immediately ordered such a real heavy rain on the area that all its streams, lakes, and pools remained full with water for many years to come, and all the birds, and animals of the jungle including the deer lived happily ever after.

(Based on the story told to the author, by his mother)

8. Evil Doesn't Go Unpunished

It is said that once upon a time, there lived two weavers in a small village. One of them was, a very honest hard working, and God worshipping guy, who always used to weave beautiful bed sheets and carpets with the best kind of cotton thread, he could find. He used to charge his customers, a very fair price, irrespective of their age or social status, and would daily go to worship and light small clay lamps in the village temple, which was dedicated to Hindu god Shiva.

However, the other guy was an exact opposite. He was the most dishonest person, and would not miss any opportunity to cheat his customers and sell them lower quality carpets, at high prices. He didn't believe in any god either, what to speak of doing any worship, or lighting any lamps in a temple, he used to stealthily follow the good guy to the temple, and as soon as the good guy left the temple, he would throw stones at the lamps, to break or extinguish them.

He had mastered the art of marketing. Since the most of the customers for the bed sheets and carpets, used to come from the nearby cities, he would chose very suitable locations near the bus stop or the railway station, and display his good quality sheets and carpets on a high pedestal, but would pass on the lower quality wares to the unwitting customers.

However the honest weaver, did not know any such tactics, he would simply wait in his house for the local customers to come and buy, what they needed. So in a short time, the dishonest weaver became quite rich and affluent, and the honest weaver was barely able to survive. But still, he did not leave his honesty, and faith in God, and kept on regularly going to the temple, doing the worship and lighting the lamps.

One day it so happened, that a very heavy hail and thunder storm, accompanied by a vey high velocity wind raged in the village. Since the poor good guy did not have any good umbrella, his wife convinced him to skip going to the temple for this day, and do his worship and light the lamp at his home, keeping god Shiva in mind.

But the dishonest weaver thought that the good guy would never miss going to the temple, and lighting the lamps, therefore he must go and break the lamps. However, when he went there, he saw no light coming from there, so he entered inside, thinking that the good guy must have placed his lamps in some secure covered place. While he was still searching for the lighted lamps, it is said that god Shiva was awakened, and in his simplicity thought that this guy is a true devotee of his, who had come to worship him even in this terrible weather. Therefore, in his divine voice, he said: " O my devotee, I have been very much pleased by your steadfast devotion, and worship even in such difficult circumstances, so ask for any boon you want."

Since this guy was a weaver, he immediately asked for a boon of additional one hundred hands, so that he could make many bed sheets and carpets at the same time. God Shiva immediately granted this wish of his, and he started happily towards his home with one hundred hands dangling from his body.

By this time, the storm had stalled, and the villagers came out of their houses, and were walking towards the temple, and assessing the damage on the way. But then from a distance, they saw this strange creature walking towards them, with so many hands dangling from its body. Since they had never seen such a creature before, they thought, that this is some dragon with an evil spirit, who is responsible for this terrible storm, and huge damage to the village. Therefore, lest this creature does more harm, they immediately started hitting it with stones, and killed him on the spot.

It is said that this evil guy was hit by as many stones, as he had thrown at the lighted lamps, and thus ultimately was punished for his evil deeds.

(Adapted from a story, the author heard in school from his divinity teacher).

9. How Much Land Does A Man Need?

Once in a village in Punjab, India there lived a farmer, named Bahadur Singh. He had inherited a small one acre piece of land from his father, He was a hard working young man and was living a happy contented life, living on the income derived from the food grains, and vegetables, which he would grow every year on his land. In fact in a few years, he was able to save enough money, and could afford to marry a young beautiful girl from a neighboring village.

In a few years, this couple gave birth to three children, and started to feel that the land they had was not enough for feeding and educating their children. So they started to work more hard, and tried to save as much money as they could, and one day were able to buy additional ½ acre of land from their neighbor. They thought that this would provide enough income to them to adequately take care and educate their children. But unluckily, due to two, three consecutive years of droughts, even their expanded farm was not sufficient to provide enough income for their family. Moreover, due to growth in population, and accelerated urbanization, the land prices had suddenly increased at an alarming rate, so they could not afford to buy any additional land, with their meager savings.

Therefore, Bahadur Singh started enquiring about other possibilities in the country. To his surprise, he found out that far off in the state of Assam, land was being sold by some *Adivassies* (ab-originals), at dirt-cheap rates. Many of his acquaintances had gone there, and bought big chunks of fertile land at very nominal prices, and were living happily there. So Bahadur Singh also decided to go and try his luck there.

After many days of tiring journey by train, bus, horse buggy, and walking on bare feet, he reached the head quarter of the *Adivassies*, met their chief, and enquired if he has more land available to sell, and what was the rate per acre. The *Adivassies* chief told Bahadur Singh, that in fact, he has much more land to sell, and as for the rate per acre, they don't know any such thing. What they do is that they go to the starting point of their land, the buyer deposits a fixed some of money, and as soon as the sun rises, he starts marking the boundary of his land, with any sharp tool, and tries to encircle as much land, as he can, but makes sure that, he reaches back at the starting point, before the sun set. If he reaches before sunset, all the land marked by him becomes his, but if he does not reach the starting point, before sunset, then he does not get any land and loses all his deposit.

Bahadur Singh accepted these terms, and next day, accompanied the *Adivassies* to the starting point. He quickly looked at the available land, and felt very happy in his mind that this was truly a very fertile land, and he could easily cover a big chunk in the duration of the day. So he immediately deposited the required sum of money with the chief of *Adivassies*, and started waiting impatiently for the sun to rise.

As soon as he saw the first ray of sun, and got a nod from the chief, Bahadur Singh immediately proceeded on his task of marking the land, and walking swiftly to the next point.

He soon found out that as he proceeded farther and farther, the land appeared more and more productive and fertile, so he kept on enlarging his boundary wider and wider. In this way, he covered a very vast area, but when he looked at the sun, he noticed that, the day was almost 3/4th gone, and it was already the afternoon. So he started walking and marking very fast, and going towards the starting point. However on the way, he would suddenly come across some extraordinary fertile plots of land, which his greed won't let him pass without marking. With the result that when he once again looked at the sky, he noticed that, the sun was about to set in a few minutes. So he immediately girded his loins, and started running as fast as he could, while dragging his marking tool behind him. As he came near the starting point, he noticed that the Adivassies were cheering him, for being such a strong person, and covering so much land in the day, which no one had done before. But as for Bahadur Singh, his lips were absolutely dry, his heart was throbbing at a very high rate, and he was feeling excruciating pain in his chest. Still, ignoring all these discomforts, Bahadur Singh, made a last ditch effort, and before the last ray of the sun could disappear, he made a big leap, fell down on the ground, extended his hand, and touched the starting peg.

At this point, all the Adivassies, started making many more joyous noises. But when their chief bent over Bahadur Singh, to help him sit down, he noticed that a big foam was coming out from His mouth, and his body was lifeless. All the Adivassies tried to revive him, as best as they could, but ultimately gave up, and started digging a pit, only about two and half yards long, and about one and a half yard wide, and this was ultimately, all the land Bahadur Singh needed.

(Adapted from a story, which the author read in his high school, which was adapted from a Russian story by Leo Tolstoy).

CONCLUSION

The author hopes that the above quotes and stories from different religions and traditions would be enough to convince the readers that even though religions may be different and diverse in many respects, yet they all teach us to practice some basic good values and virtues, such as truth, honesty, love, compassion, and kindness, and avoid some obvious sins and evils, such as lust, anger, greed, ego, and slander, and this is the unity in the diversity of different religions, and this is what we need to share with our friends and family, and teach our children.